Inside the US Air Force

Jennifer Boothroyd

Lerner Publications • Minneapolis

For United States
Air Force families

Lerner Publications Company
A division of Lerner Publishing Group, Inc.
241 First Avenue North
Minneapolis, MN 55401 USA

For reading levels and more information, look up this title at www.lernerbooks.com.

Library of Congress Cataloging-in-Publication Data

Names: Boothroyd, Jennifer, 1972- author.
Title: Inside the US Air Force / Jennifer Boothroyd.
Description: Minneapolis : Lerner Publications, [2017] | Series: Lightning bolt books. US Armed
    Forces | Includes bibliographical references and index. | Audience: Grades K-3.
Identifiers: LCCN 2016038206 (print) | LCCN 2016038342 (ebook) | ISBN 9781512433920
    (library binding : alk. paper) | ISBN 9781512450668 (eb pdf)
Subjects: LCSH: United States. Air Force—Juvenile literature.
Classification: LCC UG633 .B665 2017 (print) | LCC UG633 (ebook) | DDC 358.400973—dc23

LC record available at https://lccn.loc.gov/2016038206

Manufactured in the United States of America
1-42028-23898-9/27/2016

Table of Contents

What is the US Air Force?

The US military protects the country and its citizens. The air force is the military branch responsible for air and space defense.

Airman is the job title for most men and women who work for the air force.

The airmen who track hurricanes are nicknamed Hurricane Hunters.

The air force gathers pictures of enemy troops from above. It moves US troops and supplies around the world. The air force also tracks hurricanes.

This student attends school on a US Air Force base in Japan.

There are US Air Force bases all around the world. Bases are like special towns. People in the air force live and work there.

Air Force Training

People in the air force must complete basic training. Most train at Lackland Air Force Base in Texas.

These trainees are at Lackland.

This future airman trains for up to sixteen hours a day.

For eight and a half weeks, trainees learn the rules all airmen must follow. They learn first aid skills, rifle skills, and combat skills. They train hard to become physically fit.

The hardest part of basic training is BEAST week. During this week, the trainees live as if they are in a war. They use all the skills they have learned to protect their camp.

Trainees work together during BEAST week. *BEAST* stands for Basic Expeditionary Airman Skills Training.

There are many jobs in the air force. Airmen can be firefighters, computer programmers, and mechanics.

After completing basic training, trainees graduate as airmen. The airmen learn what jobs they will have. They get special training for those jobs.

Airmen who want to become pilots need extra training. They use computers to practice flying before they get to do it in real life.

Flying a plane is a lot of responsibility.

Air Force Equipment

Airmen need gear to do their jobs safely. Many airmen wear ear protection while working.

Airplanes can be loud. Airmen protect their ears from the noise.

G suits keep jet pilots from fainting.

Jet pilots fly fast. They wear G suits, or anti-gravity suits, to keep blood moving in their bodies when flying.

Air force jet pilots also wear masks while they fly. The masks help them breathe.

The air force has many amazing machines. Some fighter jets can fly faster than the speed of sound. That means they can go more than 768 miles (1,236 kilometers) per hour!

A C-5 Galaxy is very big. It can carry tanks and helicopters!

Transports are planes used to move equipment. One type of transport is the C-5 Galaxy.

The Air Force of the Future

The air force looks for new ways to keep its airmen and the country safe. In the future, air and space planes may have lasers that shoot away any danger.

Lasers like this one may someday protect air force planes.

Future air and space planes may be able to fly long missions without a pilot inside. The X-37B is a new space plane the air force has been testing.

The X-37B has spent almost two years in space without a pilot inside.

All parts of the US Air Force work together to protect our country.

Jet Fighter Pilot Gear Diagram

harness

flight suit

G suit

helmet

oxygen mask

boots

US Air Force History

- The US Air Force wasn't officially created until 1947. Before then, pilots were part of the US Army.

- The US military bought the world's first military airplane in 1909. It was built by Wilbur and Orville Wright.

- Women were first trained as US Air Force pilots in the early 1940s during World War II (1939-1945).

Glossary

airman: a member of the air force

combat: active fighting in a war

defense: resistance against attack

hurricane: a spinning storm formed in the water with strong winds that is usually accompanied by rain, thunder, and lightning

mission: a job, or task, to accomplish

trainee: a person who is training to become a member of the US Air Force

Further Reading

Caulkins, Sam. *My Uncle Is in the Air Force.* New York: PowerKids, 2016.

Lusted, Marcia Amidon. *Air Commandos: Elite Operations.* Minneapolis: Lerner Publications, 2014.

Murray, Julie. *United States Air Force.* Minneapolis: Abdo Kids, 2015.

National Museum of the US Air Force
http://www.nationalmuseum.af.mil/Education/ForKids.aspx

Nova: Outfitting a Fighter Pilot
http://www.pbs.org/wgbh/nova/military/pilot-gear.html

Silverman, Buffy. *How Do Jets Work?* Minneapolis: Lerner Publications, 2013.

Index

Photo Acknowledgments

The images in this book are used with the permission of: U.S. Air Force photo/Senior Airman Brett Clashman, pp. 2, 15; U.S. Air Force photo/Staff Sgt. Marc I. Lane, p. 4; U.S. Air Force photo/Staff Sgt. Mike Meares, p. 5; U.S. Air Force photo by Staff Sgt. Marie Brown, p. 6; © Ron S Buskirk/Alamy, p. 7; U.S. Air Force photo/Staff Sgt. Natasha Stannard, p. 8; U.S. Air Force photo by David Terry, p. 9; U.S. Air Force photo/Tech. Sgt. Robert Cloys, p. 10; U.S. Air Force photo/Tech. Sgt. Chris Hibben, p. 11; U.S. Air Force photo by Senior Airman Victor J. Caputo/Released, p. 12; DoD photo by Senior Airman Gustavo Castillo, U.S. Air Force/Released, p. 13; U.S. Air Force photo/Staff Sgt. Joe W. McFadden, p. 14; U.S. Air Force photo/Roland Balik, p. 16; © Edwards Air Force Base/RGB Ventures/SuperStock/Alamy, p. 17; U.S. Air Force photo by Michael Stonecypher, p. 18; U.S. Air Force photo/Senior Airman Nesha Humes, p. 19; © US Navy Photo/Alamy, p. 20; U.S. Air Force archive photo, p. 21; U.S. Air Force photo/Osakabe Yasuo, p. 23.

Front cover: U.S. Air Force photo/Tech. Sgt. Jason Robertson.

Main body text set in Billy Infant regular 28/36. Typeface provided by SparkType.